WISE CHOICES

TRUE OR FALSE:
Thinking correctly about new spirituality

PETER JONES

> 'Get wisdom, get understanding; do not forget my words
> or swerve from them.
> Do not forsake wisdom, and she will protect you; love her,
> and she will watch over you.
> Wisdom is supreme; therefore get wisdom.
> Though it cost all you have, get understanding.'
>
> *Proverbs 4:5-7*

© Day One Publications

This UK edition, printed 2007

All Scripture quotations are taken from the author's direct translation

A CIP record is held at The British Library   ISBN 978-1-84625-049-1

Published by Day One Publications Ryelands Road, Leominster, HR6 8NZ

☎ 01568 613 740 FAX 01568 611 473 email—sales@dayone.co.uk www.dayone.co.uk

All rights reserved

No part of this publication may be reproduced, or stored in a retrieval system, or transmitted, in any form or by any means, mechanical, electronic, photocopying, recording or otherwise, without the prior permission of Day One Publications

Editor (this UK edition) Jim Holmes

Design: Steve Devane Illustrations: www.donkeyworks.com London, England

True or false UK EDITION OF GOSPEL TRUTH PAGAN LIES, CAN YOU TELL THE DIFFERENCE? PETER JONES, MAIN ENTRY EDITIONS, ESCONDIDO, CA 92025, COPYRIGHT 1999, 2004

Printed by Gutenberg Press, Malta

CONTENTS

A NOTE FROM THE AUTHOR	5
NEW WINDS?	6
THE FIVE POINTS OF MONISM	10
PAGAN LIE 1: ALL IS ONE AND ONE IS ALL	13
GOSPEL TRUTH 1: ONE GOD, THE CREATOR	17
PAGAN LIE 2: HUMANITY IS ONE	20
GOSPEL TRUTH 2: ONE IN CHRIST ALONE	23
PAGAN LIE 3: ALL RELIGIONS ARE ON	27
GOSPEL TRUTH 3: ONE TRUTH	30
PAGAN LIE 4: ONE PROBLEM: AMNESIA	33
GOSPEL TRUTH 4: ONE PROBLEM: DEATH THROUGH SIN	40
PAGAN LIE 5: ONE ESCAPE: LOOK WITHIN	43
GOSPEL TRUTH 5: ONE ESCAPE: LOOK TO HIM	47
GOSPEL TRUTH, PAGAN LIES AND YOU	54
SUMMARY: PAGAN LIES	56
SUMMARY: GOSPEL TRUTH	57
BY THE SAME AUTHOR	59

Commendations

'**Peter Jones is on the cutting edge of culture. This book cuts to the chase on the issue of the viability of the truth of Christianity in the midst of paganism.**'–John MacArthur, Pastor-Teacher, Grace Community Church, Sun Valley, California

'**Wonderfully insightful... A great youth group study book or a gift for young adults or sceptics about Christianity. Even mature middle-school children would find this a complete overview to equip them to evaluate many of our culture's messages in the light of the Bible.**'— Linda Harvey, Editor, Mission America

'**...easy enough for older children, deep enough for mature adults. Parents and teachers will find this book one of the most valuable resources for leading others to the truth.**'—Rosemary Jensen, Executive Director, Bible Study Fellowship International

A note from the author

Pagan? Do you recoil at my use of such a term? 'Pagan' comes from the Latin, *paganus*, 'of the earth'. Those who call themselves pagans happily admit to worshipping the earth. The mass-marketing of their pagan spirituality proceeds with hardly a word of dissent. Have you noticed the New Age section in your local chain bookstore getting bigger by the month—hundreds of books on witchcraft and the worship of the goddess, the self, animals and nature? In my local store, I looked in vain for books from another perspective. The saleswoman pointed me to the Religion section. But no help there. The few Christian books on the shelf did not deal with the issue, and the other religious publications were filled with pagan assumptions.

I wrote this book to fill the gap. As you read, you will discover the difference between worshipping the God who made the earth and worshipping the earth itself. Once you've understood that difference, you must decide in all honesty if you are a pagan or a Christian.

New winds?

I couldn't believe my eyes. On the platform of the vast ballroom in the Palmer House Hotel in downtown Chicago, stood representatives of 125 world religions, assembled for the Parliament of the World's Religions. A liberal Presbyterian professor in his long black robe; a Buddhist priest in his orange one; a Catholic cardinal in his royal purple splendour; the high priestess of the goddess Isis in her white robe and pointed headdress—all stood together in celebration of their spiritual unity.

Having just returned from eighteen years in France, where it was impolite to talk religion in public, I was faced with an America I had never seen before. I knew America has always been spiritual, but in 1993 in Chicago, I saw a new kind of spirituality that joined all the religions of the world.

We have never lived in a more spiritual time
People are waking up to their spiritual potential. Gurus propose techniques for prayer and meditation that they claim will bring us into communion with our higher selves and the god within. Today witches, chiropractors, yoga instructors—even cereal manufacturers—all claim to be spiritual.

Christians find themselves confused. No longer faced with a takeover by atheistic Communists, they are not sure if they even have an enemy. Enemies are not in vogue in a society of tolerance. Aren't all 'people of faith' on the same side? The cold war is over; democracy and material ease are spreading to cover most of the globe. Hope of a new dawn for humanity hovers in the air of a new millennium, and atheists are mostly a thing of the past. Ninety-seven per cent of Americans believe in God. Ninety per cent of these believe God loves them. In the UK and in Europe generally people are spiritual but not religious. With all this spirituality, one would expect social harmony and moral excellence. Strangely, the very opposite is the case!

Since the sixties, spiritual America has become a world leader in pornography, juvenile crime, abortion, divorce, cohabitation, adultery, family breakdown, radical feminism and militant homosexuality. If so many people believe in God, why such social and personal disintegration? What kind of god condones such selfish and immoral behaviour?

We have never lived in a more spiritually confusing time
TimeLIFE Books promotes *The American Indians*, with the following invitation: 'Come to a place where spirits are real.' The Bible calls us to spiritual discernment. We are not to 'believe every spirit, but test the spirits to see if they are from God' (1 John 4:1). We need to wake up. Anti-Christian but very spiritual paganism is flooding the west.

- Two thousand women from mainline churches met in Minneapolis in 1993 to 're-imagine' their Christian faith. They mocked the God of the Bible and worshipped the goddesses of ancient paganism.

- Every autumn, tens of thousands of otherwise normal Americans meet at the Burning Man Festival in the Nevada desert to worship Papa Satan.

You might argue that only oddballs or the intellectual elite believe in this kind of spirituality. But if your shopping centre is like the one near me, you can walk into a young woman's clothing store, where my thirteen year old thinks the clothes are 'rad', and where teens discover an entire bookshelf on witchcraft, or buy badges declaring, 'I love eternal damnation', and 'I am God'. Do you sense the dark waters rising? We will drown if we do not realize what is happening. As our ship of state sails straight for an iceberg, are we on deck playing shovelboard?

The title of a book promoting witchcraft, *The Changing of the Gods*, aptly describes what has happened since the generation of the sixties. Many believe in god, but they no longer believe in the one exclusive God revealed in the Bible. We are now comfortable with *many* gods.

The Bible calls a warning to us. There are only two kinds of spirituality—Christian or pagan. The two systems have nothing in common, and are as different as the truth and the lie. But paganism loves to disguise itself in Christian clothes. It tells us that Christianity is part of a global unity, and that paganism is the true expression of what Jesus taught. Don't believe it. To step into the pagan circle, you have to set Christian thinking aside.

This book deals in ground-zero thinking. It explains:

1. how the spirituality around us is often pagan and anti-Christian, and how the seemingly unrelated radical agenda are, underneath, aspects of this pagan way of looking at the world;

2. how Christian spirituality differs in every respect from pagan spirituality, though the pagan sometimes dresses in Christian clothes.

If you are a Christian, I hope what I write here will help you to avoid being 'blown here and there by every wind of teaching and by the cunning and craftiness of men in their deceitful scheming' (Ephesians 4:14). Paganism comes in many forms. Some are clearly anti-Christian. Others claim to be Christian. We need a clear grasp of biblical truth and of the system that falsely claims to be the truth.

If you are not a Christian, I respect your search for true spirituality and your willingness to read this book. I encourage you to open your mind to the God who made you and calls you to love him. I pray that what I write will provoke you to search for the Christ of the Bible, and to realize that any spirituality which fails to proclaim Jesus (born, crucified and raised) is ultimately no spirituality at all.

Whether you are a Christian or not, I warn you of the stakes. The devil's lies are clever, intended to mislead. He doesn't bother with the kind of lie my brother-in-law once told as a child, when his dad discovered the cause of a short circuit: a nail stuck into the bathroom wall socket. 'It just fell in, dad!' he lamely suggested. The devil's lies address real human needs and offer seemingly plausible solutions. They worked on Adam and Eve and were tried with great finesse on Jesus.

Our culture offers us an attractive array of spiritual solutions to society's problems and to our own loneliness and emptiness. But before we follow any path, we must understand where it will take us, remembering paganism's ultimate goal—the subversion of God's truth.

So as you read this booklet, keep asking yourself this simple question: 'Gospel truth, pagan lies—can *I* tell the difference?'

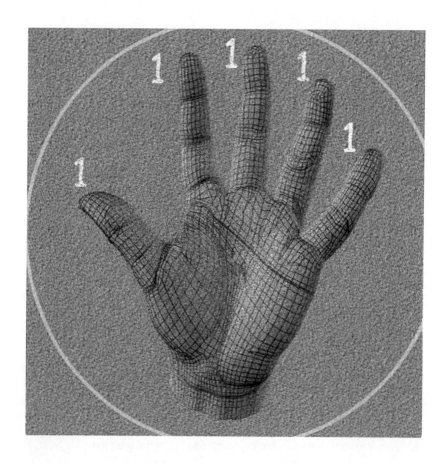

The five points of monism

I met my wife in the late sixties in Boston, where long-haired hippies camped out on the Boston common on a spiritual high through drugs or Eastern meditation. We dismissed them as failed revolutionaries on the edges of society. But in the 21st century, we see that their revolution has succeeded. They introduced Hindu religion into the once Christian West. The average person now accepts ideas like transcendental meditation, New Age spirituality, many paths to God, or oneness with the divine universe.

These notions are pagan lies. As I mentioned earlier, the word 'pagan' comes from the Latin, *paganus*, 'of the earth'. The Apostle Paul gives us God's definition of a pagan: someone who 'changes the truth of God for the lie and worships and serves the creature rather than the Creator' (Romans 1:25).

These two notions of worship are opposites. They cannot be blended together. One is truth; the other is a counterfeit. The words *worship* and *serve* show that a pagan is spiritual. We are all dedicated to something in which we believe and according to which we behave. Everyone is spiritual. If we worship and serve anything other than God the only Creator and Redeemer, we are pagans, whether we like the term or not.

'You gotta serve somebody,' sang Dylan. 'It may be the devil or it may be the Lord,' the maker of heaven and earth. If it is the devil, he will get you to worship the earth in one form or another.

'We do not fight against human beings,' said the apostle Paul. 'We fight against … the rulers of the darkness of this age' (Ephesians 6:12). God is the author of Gospel truth, so the devil is the author of pagan lies. The real conflict is not with people (who may still be reached by the truth), but with the delusions they believe. As the Bible says, 'Some follow deceiving spirits and things taught by demons' (1 Timothy 4:1). Our conflict is with the devil, the father of lies, who 'deceives the whole world' (Rev. 12:9). People may repeat the lies with conviction, but as Billy Graham has often said, 'You can be sincere, but sincerely wrong.'

I call today's paganism *monism*. The word *paganism* evokes various non-Christian religions and cults, whereas *monism* reminds us of their common core. If you take the *m* off, you get *one-ism*. This booklet describes five principles of monism to help you identify spiritual falsehood. After each point, I have included a chapter on the corresponding Gospel truth. Parents may wish to help their children find examples of each point in the areas of school, friends, and society. The questions at the end of each chapter will help you discuss how to explain and to live the Christian faith.

The opposite of monism is Christian *theism*, which I also call two-ism, that is, the biblical view of reality where there are two kinds of existence, ours and God's. As you can see these are two fundamentally opposed worldviews, one called monism/one-ism, the other called theism/two-ism. The faith revealed in the Bible is theistic, honouring God as Lord of all. God (*theos* in Greek) and the universe are distinct, like a watch and a watchmaker, or, to use a biblical image, like a potter and his clay. The other is monistic, seeing god merely as a 'divine' but impersonal force or 'energy field' in everything and everybody.

Of course no one is consistent. Pagans borrow Christian ideas, and Christians don't always think as theists. Paganism is like a downward spiral. In the vortex at the bottom is Satan and worship of evil. Most people stand at the outer edges, but the sweep begins to carry them downwards. Biblical theism is like an upward spiral that brings us into the light of God's presence. Believers stand at various levels of the spiral. But if you try to put one foot in each spiral, you will be in a most uncomfortable contortion that causes great confusion. Either you are caught up in the Spirit of God through Christ and you are being swept upwards, or you are caught up in the spirit of the earth and you are headed downwards.

Let's get back to spiritual ground zero, and take a look at the two spirals, the two worldviews.

PAGAN LIE 1

All is one and one is all

Here is a rather obvious American example of the infiltration into everyday politics of religious paganism. In 1998, a woman representing the Natural Law party ran for Secretary of State in California. Government, she believes, is the 'reflection of collective consciousness, and needs a unifying principle ... of harmony, positivity and wholeness, in which no one can go wrong and everyone will be spontaneously right.' To attain this wholeness, she proposed a programme of 'education to develop higher states of consciousness.'

You can see that pagan monism is not just theory. Such spirituality is already part of national politics. Because paganism relates to this world, and not the world to come, religious paganism actually must take on political form, as the Bible indicates (Revelation 17). This unifying principle of wholeness is another form of one-ism. This is why monism loves the symbolism of the inclusive circle.

In the Disney movie, *Lion King*, everything in the universe is a part of a mass of energy. There is no Creator: the circle of life swallows up God. Many non-Christian faiths use circles as a means of expressing this all-is-one philosophy. Hinduism, goddess worship, New Age/Taoist physics, witchcraft, and the Parliament of the World's Religions all show universal unity with circles. This circular, all-is-one notion inspires deep ecology and the worship of bewitching, encircling Mother Earth.

A young adult novel that recently came across my desk echoes this Mother Earth-oneness spirituality. Says the American Indian who serves as spiritual guide to the young hero:

> It is the same for all things: small circles of individual life and spirit within the big circle which is the pattern of all life, all spirit ... We must remember the circle that holds all things.

A similar notion appears in the movie *Star Wars*. Obiwan Kenobi, the Jedi warrior, explains to young Luke Skywalker, in language like that of a pagan priest or priestess:

> The Force is an energy field created by all living things: it surrounds us, penetrates us; it binds the galaxy together...it is all-powerful [and] controls everything.

When Luke abandons himself to his intuitions, he is able, in harmony with the Force, to pilot a complex flying machine in a pinpoint bombing of the headquarters of the Evil Empire. If you believe that you might just believe anything.

Some who claim to be Christians argue that our thinking is too linear. The goddess or Mother Earth should be *restored* to Christianity. Because Mother Earth is everything, we shouldn't see things as opposites, but as different sides of the same thing. Could we not simply bring an end to conflict by changing the way we think? So in *Star Wars* the dark side of the Force is not evil, but just the other side, like the Yin and the Yang of Buddhism. George Lucas, director of *Star Wars*, said he made it to introduce Buddhism to the West.

These are spiritual ideas, but are they true spirituality?

By considering God and his creation as part of the same circle, monism leads to a confusion not only about who (or what!) God is, but also about the identity of human beings, and their place in the world.

QUESTIONS

- Where does *one-ism* show up in school, in the work place, and in public life?

- Think of movies you have seen, such as *Lion King, Powder,* or *Pocahontas*. What is the relationship between the earth and the people who live on it? Think of other movies with similar themes.

- In what ways do you see earth-worship growing? What is the difference between worshipping the earth and caring for it? (See Romans 1:25; Isaiah 51:6; Leviticus 25:23; 2 Chronicles 36:20–21.)

- How does evolution influence our thinking about the earth?

- How is God made part of the creation in the non-Christian religions you know?

- In what way is monism unbiblical? (See Job 28:12–28; Genesis 1:1; Exodus 20:3–4; Isaiah 55:8–9.)

GOSPEL TRUTH 1

One God, the Creator

To represent God and the rest of reality, monism draws one, all-inclusive circle. Theism draws two circles: a smaller circle represents everything except God, and a larger circle represents God himself. You could call this two-ism. Christians do not believe that God is his creation. God had no beginning. Creation did. Even if we could understand all there is to know about creation, we would never fully discover God. That is why the Bible warns us not to worship the creation, but to worship and serve the only one worthy of worship, the Creator. The starting point of Gospel truth is that God the Creator, in the three persons of the divine Trinity—Father, Son and Holy Spirit—is the one and only God, and that all which is not God was created by him.

The Christian faith maintains a separateness between God and his creation. We will never become God, and God remains the sovereign Lord. God says to Israel, 'You thought I was altogether like you' (Psalm 50:21), and reminds them: 'my thoughts are not your thoughts, neither are your ways my ways' (Isaiah 55:8). Of course Christians do become united to God, in a personal relationship comparable to marriage. As in marriage, neither abandons his or her identity in the union of deep love.

Unlike monism, the Christian faith can explain why human beings are people and not rocks; why we can sing, love, paint and write poetry. God is personal and made men and women to reflect his personal nature. When we listen to God's written Word of revelation we discover the path he opens for us to become united to him in eternal love.

I once stood before a glorious, shimmering waterfall with a friend who believes God is too great to be personal. We both had an overwhelming sense of worship as we stood awed by the sparkling wall of water that hung half-frozen in the crisp air. 'You have a very comfortable position as a Christian,' said my friend. And he was right. Christians are at home in the universe. God made us. God made everything else, and he put us here to know and please him.

The church acknowledges God's supreme position in its confession 'to God alone be the glory':

Soli Deo Gloria

QUESTIONS

- How do you know, from the Bible, that God is separate from what he made? (See Genesis 1:1; Job 41:10–11; Psalm 24:1–2; 30:1–6, 10–12.)

- How can we acknowledge God's distinct character in our church worship and in our daily lives? (See Proverbs 3:5–6; Revelation 4:11; 5:12–13.)

- If we are not a part of the earth, why should we be concerned about it? (See Genesis 1:28; Hosea 4:1–3.)

- Can a Christian use alternative medicine? What if the practitioner claims that the body is the source of healing? In what way is this true? In what way is it false? (See Hosea 11:3–4; Acts 8:9–24; James 5:14–16.)

- What other decisions might be affected by the fact that we are distinct from God?

PAGAN LIE 2

Humanity is one

The Baha'i Club (a religion that seeks to join all religions) at UC Davis (the University of California) uses a circle within a circle. Around the circle we read: 'God is one; humanity is one; all religions are one.' This second principle of monism flows naturally from the first. If all is one and one is all, then humanity is a part of God, an expression of divine oneness. Humans are a kind of concentrated cosmic energy who create their own reality. Belief that humans are divine, and essentially good, explains today's quest for personal spiritual discovery and the hope that we can create heaven on earth. This monistic humanism becomes a very attractive path to religious and social utopia.

Already in a 1983 issue of the *Humanist* we see a deeply religious view of humanism replacing atheism. The article asks classroom teachers to wage a battle for the future of humanity. 'The classroom must become an arena of conflict between the old and the new—the rotting corpse of Christianity ... and the new faith of humanism, resplendent with its promise of a world in which the never-realized Christian ideal of 'love thy neighbour' will finally be achieved.' By finding God in ourselves, monists hope to break down the divisions in our world and accomplish God's loving work by uniting with one another.

If we are little holograms of divinity—smaller, cloned versions of the great divine circle—then we are uncreated and eternal. We are as old as God! We are outside the jurisdiction of any authority—a kingless generation. What need have we to submit to outside rule? If we are God, if we are as old as God, then we can make our own rules.

We also decide our own truth. Each person contributes his piece of truth by constructing his own version of reality. When it all comes together, it makes some kind of mystical, nonsensical sense. This explains why tolerance is so important. Each self is a source of truth, so each must be tolerated, even encouraged.

This monistic thinking explains such programmes as 'values clarification' taught in many public schools where children are encouraged to create their own personal reality and to accept their own inner identity as divine. They must thus abandon themselves to what feels right, including their own sexual urges. This is the correct way to 'learn' because the individual is hailed as the final judge of all. Intuition is the inviting bridge over which we stroll, in calm self-affirmation, into human freedom and into oneness with the universe.

Monism refuses a system that creates categories and makes distinctions. Of course, monism, in spite of its claim to tolerance, also creates distinctions—especially between those who agree that there is only one circle and those who don't. There isn't much place for Christians in this soft but suffocating circle!

QUESTIONS

- What are some signs of global unity today?

- Should Christians resist or fear forms of globalism—cultural, commercial, financial, political and religious? (See Psalm 24:1; Matthew 28:19–20; Acts 13:47; Revelation 11:15.)

- What are the implications of the growing, evil alliance between religion and politics? Will the church triumph? What experiences might Christians have? (See Psalm 2; Joel 3; Revelation 13:5–10; 20:7–10.)

- Are we close to this time of global unity? (See Mark 13:10; Luke 21:24; Romans 11:25; Revelation 13:11–17; 17:15–17.)

GOSPEL TRUTH 2

One in Christ alone

The Bible teaches that all humans are created by God. In this sense, all humanity is equal. No human being has intrinsically more value than another in God's eyes. But there is a distinction between people. Some are not only God's creatures, but his children. This truth has become offensive to most people; no one likes the idea that some might be left out of the family. But children of God recognize him as the Creator, distinct from his creation. They have accepted his revelation of himself in his word as well as his offer of forgiveness that erases their sin, and have placed their faith in Jesus, his Son. They have come to God not on their own terms, but on his.

Non-Christians think Christians are proud when they create these categories between people. However, each Christian knows that if he has been adopted into God's family, it is only by God's undeserved kindness. There is no pride in faith. Faith is simply the belief that we can do nothing to save ourselves, but that we rely utterly on the gift of God. So, this definition of family is made not in pride, but in humility. What could be proud about admitting you are not God?

Does pride not characterize rather the person who sees himself as divine, and determines for himself what is true and false? A Christian receives truth from a God to whom he submits his finite understanding. A pagan creates his own truth, pretending to interpret the world from the throne he has usurped from the Creator. In Jeremiah we read: 'Every man's own word becomes his oracle and so you distort the words of the living God' (Jeremiah 23:36). Here we see the difference between Christianity and paganism. Through his Word, God defines truth to his people. Pagans define it for themselves.

Today we hear a lot of talk about multi-culturalism. Because our globe has become so small, we are beginning to realize that all men and women share the same joys and sorrows, the same struggle against disease and disaster, and the same desire for a happier life. However, true unity can only come in Christ. I do not mean to imply that only Christians know how to be kind to others, or to take a stand of self-sacrifice. Some Christians fall terribly short of the love God makes possible, and some non-Christians are generous and helpful. But we must define unity as God defines it, not as we would like to see it. God is the only one who can see and judge the motives of our hearts.

God divides people into two categories: those who believe on his Son Jesus Christ, for whom there is no condemnation, and those who are condemned by their lack of belief (John 3:18). Those who belong to Jesus will live in perfect harmony for ever in the kingdom he is preparing. Christians are not one with pagans, for each serves a different master.

We once had the misfortune of falling into the hands of a successful timeshare salesman. As he painted a rosy picture of fun in the sun, he held a crumpled piece of paper on which he had scribbled some mistaken calculations. I could tell he was longing to get rid of it. The conversation had turned for a moment to the Christian faith. I said to him, 'Tony, the Christian faith is like this: You have some rubbish there in your hand that you're longing to get rid of. Now, think of that rubbish as your sin. Suppose I make you a deal. I'll take the rubbish and give you this deed for a perfect holiday home, where you'll have a lot more than one week every other year. You can live there for ever with those who love you most. What about it? Want to do business?'

Tony laughed. And so do we all, at first, when we hear the conditions of the deal Jesus offers us. Give up our rubbish to inherit the kingdom? It seems too good to be true, yet Christians are those who have 'fallen for' the deal. By the way, we did buy the timeshare, and yes, we do regret it! But we do not regret having humbled ourselves enough to exchange our crumpled calculations for a deed to Jesus' kingdom. Only he unlocks the door to his kingdom. This is why the church confesses 'Christ alone':

Solus Christus

QUESTIONS

- How do you understand multiculturalism—both national and international? What is the scriptural basis for humans to find unity? (See Acts 17:24–31; Isaiah 2, 55:1–5.)

- How can we honour Christ now as Lord of the universe? (See Colossians 1:15–20; Ephesians 1:3–10, 4:20–24.)

- In what ways is the Church a genuinely global and multi-cultural institution? Think about how Christians should celebrate and promote this global unity. (See Galatians 3:26–29; Ephesians 2:11–22.)

PAGAN LIE 3

All religions are one

In Chicago in 1993, delegates to the Parliament of the World's Religions held hands and danced around the room to the sound of a Native American Indian shaman's drum. Eight thousand delegates shared their experience of the divine within. If all humanity is one, then all religions are one.

Mystical oneness is at the heart of spirituality for the monist. All religions share a common, mystical experience, and true believers in any religion will arrive at the same unio mystica (mystical union with God in which we become divine). All religions are pie slices that join at the centre. If you believe in this oneness, you must throw away rationality, for mystical union is an irrational affair. If you believe in this oneness, you must throw off doctrine. It doesn't matter if you are a Christian, a Jew, a Hindu or a witch; you are a part of the same whole, which is *God*. You can find union with that whole—and the way to union is experience. Just bite into the pie!

This unity of religions will increase in the years ahead. Technology has brought our world together. In addition, many religious organizations (the World Council of Churches, the United Religions, the Parliament of the World's Religions, and the Interfaith Movement, for example) are working hard to bring about a one-world reality. A world-renowned expert in Comparative Religions, Huston Smith, believes that the present work of the Spirit is producing an 'invisible geometry to shape the religions of the world into a single truth'. Some in the established churches, including Presbyterians, Anglicans, Methodists and Baptists, believe Smith is a prophet for the church of the third millennium.

This religious one-world vision becomes political because paganism worships only the earth. Mikhail Gorbachev, the last leader of the atheistic Soviet Union, now organizes an annual State of the World Forum in San Francisco, attended by many religious and political leaders. Gorbachev has a spiritual vision for the planet. He calls for 'a new synthesis of democratic, Christian and Buddhist values'. Translated, that means a joining of Eastern and Western religions in a new global, political structure that will finally bring peace to the world. What an enticing proposition. But is it true?

QUESTIONS

- Should we avoid contact with people from non-Christian religions? (See Acts 12:16–32; Ephesians 2:1–10, 4:17–24; 1 Peter 2:9–12.)

- What are the dangers in such contacts? (See Philippians 3:12–21.)

- Is the Interfaith Movement something Christians should support? (See 2 Kings 17:24–41.)

- What spiritual practices are forbidden in Scripture? (See Exodus 22:18; Leviticus 19:26, 31; 20:6; Deuteronomy 13:1–4; 18:10–12, 22; Isaiah 47:9–13; Jeremiah 8:17; 10:2; Ezekiel 12:21f.)

GOSPEL TRUTH 3

One Truth

Some of my sixties friends turned away from drugs and Eastern mysticism to Jesus, calling themselves the Jesus People. They would point their index finger to the heavens, declaring to anyone who would listen (and to many who would rather not!) that Jesus was the only way. Normal people sneered, but when you examine things from ground zero perspective, the Jesus People were right.

The Bible teaches that there is only one true religion. All others are man-made. Jesus claims to be the only way to the Father, so he makes your attitude to him the test of true religion. Today's spirituality gives lip service to Christ, but it deforms him so that he is unrecognizable. He has become the spirit of the age, or the spirit behind Jesus—one shared by any great prophet or guru.

In the Old Testament, God's people were warned not to experiment with pagan religions, and are judged for being full of superstitions from the east, for practising divination and for clasping hands with pagans (Isaiah 2:6). Jesus told us specifically not to practise religion as the pagans did (Matthew 6:7). Christ is the only way, because he is the unique Son of God. He created the world, a unique event in our human history. Without him, nothing was made. But Christ was at the centre of another unique event when he redeemed the world. He was the first to conquer death and to wear a resurrected body. He is the first event of God's new creation.

The author of these two great acts, the physical creation and the future transformation of the universe, is the one who states: 'I am the way, the truth, and the life. No one comes to the Father except through me' (John 14:6). Before the majesty of these acts of the divine Christ, paganism stands mute. It can neither create the physical universe nor raise a dead body from the tomb.

There is only one true spirituality. Only one religion leads to God. It is the religion the true God reveals in the Bible. This is why the church confesses 'Scripture alone':

Sola Scriptura

QUESTIONS

- In speaking of the uniqueness of Christianity, how can you be bold without being obnoxious? (See Matthew 10:16; Ephesians 4:15, 25–32.)
- Does the Bible guarantee success in witness? What does it teach us about our popularity? (See Ecclesiastes 11:1; Isaiah 55:10–11; Matthew 5:11; Mark 8:34–38; Acts 5:41–42.)
- Do you think you are too bold, or too timid? Have you been mocked for your faith? What has the experience taught you? (See Matthew 5:11–12; 2 Corinthians 3:12–18; Ephesians 6:19–20.)
- Where is evangelism in your list of priorities, both your local church's list, and your own?

PAGAN LIE 4

One problem: amnesia

Most people do not think very deeply. Life is often made up of dull, unchallenging work, relieved only by the excitement of the weekly Premiership matches and 'quality time' in the pub. Is there nothing more to life? Will someone not wake them up?

The sleek, spiritually alert monists are right in wanting to awaken people from forgetfulness to spiritual reality, by which they believe they can fix the world. Monists believe that things are not as they should be. And they are right. Sadly, they don't realize that they are proposing an even greater delusion.

One might expect monism to be complacent. If all is one and one is all, what can anyone change? But monists are often passionate people who want to transform reality. Monists want to waken their brothers and sisters and the earth to the reality of universal oneness. Like the young lion, Simba in *Lion King*, the earth has not yet understood that the stars are its father.

Monism hates distinction-makers because they break the unity of the circle. Making distinctions has numbed us, they maintain, into a spiritual state of forgetfulness. We no longer remember that we belong to the whole. In order to reunite the circle, we must stop dividing the world into categories. Monism points an accusing finger at structures we once considered natural, such as a father's loving authority in his home, or a husband's loving leadership of his wife.

Monists identify old-fashioned, black and white thinking with Western Christian culture. They find the Bible full of patriarchy (male/fatherly responsibility) and hierarchy (authority structures), and they accuse Christians of making many other such distinctions which they claim tear the world apart.

Monism's message of hope is clear: we must rid the world of distinctions and enter the mystical unity of all things. Here is a partial list of distinctions that monists would like to eliminate. As you reflect on this list, you will realize many other Christian distinctions that are under attack around you.

CREATOR/CREATURE

Monism destroys the distinction between God, who existed always, and creation, which had a beginning. If the world is divine, having created itself through evolution, then we human beings can create ourselves too, evolving into a better race, with no need for a Creator. This is the major distinction which must be eliminated so that the elimination of the other distinctions can proceed without real opposition.

GOD/MAN

As in many world religions, monism believes that man is God, or at least that the sum total of all human endeavour and value equals God. Man owes no worship or obedience to a God outside creation who reveals himself to his creatures, loves them, and communicates to them in objective truth.

ANIMALS/HUMANS

What child does not love his pet? Animals hold a special place in our life and the nature in which we live is beautiful and striking. Monists rightly notice that humans often mistreat animals and destroy nature. They offer a salutary programme: eliminate the distinctions between animal, plant and human life, since everything is divine. Witches take the deification of nature to an extreme, by adopting familiars, pets that help them communicate with the spirit world.

LIFE/DEATH

Monists almost revere death for its necessary place in the circle of life. Their strong sense of the oneness of the universe is sometimes tied to a notion of reincarnation, in which the natural process of death brings them closer to perfection. Medicine now emphasizes 'dying with dignity'. Some believe that a little baby spirit knocks on the door of his mother's womb. If he hears her say, 'Not just now,' he bounces back to the world of spirit to await a more welcoming womb. The baby spirit giggles, the birds twitter, and everyone is deliriously happy!

RIGHT/WRONG

On the monistic circle, all points are relative. If you realize that your own evil is not really evil, you will know freedom. I once met a long-time church member who discovered *A Course in Miracles*. In it he read that sin did not exist and that guilt was an illusion. He testified to 'walking on air'. Many people classified as sinful, (such as pro-abortionists and homosexuals) can find a guilt-free place in society. The spiritual and mystical experience of monism frees you from a guilty conscience because your own evil is good.

HEAVEN/HELL

'Imagine there's no heaven ... [and] no hell below us,' sang my old school chum, John

Lennon, as he led the sixties generation into Eastern spirituality. Monists have no sense of a heavenly world, God's own domain, whose values and realities are beyond what we experience now. The only hell is a man-made state of judgementalism. They blame Christians for spoiling the party with their distinctions, which stir up hatred and cause suffering.

CHRIST/SATAN

Monism claims that Satan and Christ are like twins. Like the Yin and the Yang we saw earlier, they express different sides of the same reality. Because of this, monists do not value Jesus Christ's historical birth, death, resurrection and ascension, which give Christ too specific an identity. To them, the spirit of Christ is anything helpful, whether healing techniques, sexual satisfaction, or meditation. Christ and the antichrist become one and the same.

THE BIBLE/OTHER SCRIPTURES

We now find compilations of Scriptures from all the world's religions on the book store shelves. As our world goes global and as monistic thinking gains ground, you may have a hard time explaining why you trust the Bible and not other Scriptures. Since there should be no distinctions, according to monism, and since all religions are ultimately one, no revelation can claim absolute authority over us. Beside, the god within has no need of Scripture. He/she/it specializes in direct revelation without words.

SIN/HOLINESS

The very word sin has gone out of style. Even some Christian groups have begun to cringe when they find themselves using it. Monists prefer words like *wholeness* to *holiness*. They want to avoid conflict at any cost. Measuring behaviour against God's objective standards is too constraining. We will have a better chance at peace if we make up our own, less rigid standards. As long as everyone is happy about an action, it can't be wrong.

ORTHODOXY/HERESY

Even some supposedly Christian scholars want to expand the Scriptures, adding books like the Gnostic *Gospel of Thomas*. They believe there is no true or false Christian doctrine. Those who impose doctrinal standards are narrow-minded and petty. Often monists can confuse Christians by seeming to accept Christian beliefs like love and tolerance and the rejection of bigotry.

CHRISTIANITY/PAGANISM

Monists believe the distinctions between Christianity and paganism are short-sighted, mean-spirited and intolerant. Only a deep communion between all forms of spirituality—Christianity, Buddhism,

Hinduism, witchcraft, nature worship, worship of the body as a self-healing, godlike organism—can bring the world together and promote a common spirituality for the good of all.

MALE/FEMALE

Seeing such injustices as the mistreatment of women throughout the world, and violence done to homosexuals, monists propose two solutions:
1. eliminate our definition of humans as male or female, which is really a way of maintaining old-fashioned patriarchy, and
2. tolerate all sexual choices, emphasizing androgyny (being both male and female) as the ideal expression of monistic spirituality.

TRADITIONAL FAMILY/ALTERNATE FAMILIES

Monism believes the traditional family to be an obstacle to spiritual unity. We need all kinds of families: unmarried men and women living together; homosexual marriages, even 'trupples' (three homosexuals in a committed, long-term relationship). A local witch, raising her daughter with two live-in husbands, asks: 'Why should the government tell me how to run my family?' People must be free to discover their own enriching forms of relationship.

CHILD/PARENT

As more child abuse cases arise, monists suggest that the state must step in to protect them. Paganism wants to limit parental authority and eventually eliminate it, in order to free parents and to protect children. They argue that traditional family structures, especially the notion that a father is in authority over the family in any way, are dehumanizing and spiritually deadening.

AUTHORITY/SUBMISSION

When they see the misuse of authority and power in the world, monists assume that such abuse arises from the very existence of authority structures. To protect the equal value of every human being, they challenge the legitimacy of all human authority constructs, such as: teacher/student, employer/employee, parent/child, husband/wife, minister and elders/church members, etc. Monists firmly believe that radical egalitarianism and the destruction of all notions of authority and submission are keys to human happiness and social justice.

I'm sure you have seen in each of the areas just listed how monism has changed our way of thinking. What you may not have realized is that all the changes in our society are tied together. It all makes sense to a monist! Powerful forces in our world are committed to the elimination of these distinctions for the good of the planet. Of course, there is no universal human conspiracy whose headquarters are hidden under the Arizona desert, led by a Mister Big planning a pagan takeover. But behind this often alluring ideology is a *superhuman* conspiracy against God. 'For our struggle is not against human beings … but against the spiritual forces of evil in the heavenly realm' (Ephesians 6:12). The nations are caught up in this conspiracy, as Psalm 2 says: 'The kings of the earth take their stand … against the Lord and against his Anointed One.' Christians need to identify the conspiracy in order to help those caught up in it to make peace with Christ. Non-Christians are not as independent as they think. The spiritual forces of evil take delight in deceiving people in order to draw them away from Christ.

As I finished a lecture one night, a homosexual came to speak with me. Seeing anger on his face, I expected him to denounce my intolerant message. Instead, he told me how angry he was to learn that the dark forces of spiritual deception had taken him in for so long. He asked me to pray that God would rescue him from them.

'Kiss the Son, lest he be angry and you be destroyed in your way. Blessed are those who take refuge in him' (Psalm 2:12).

QUESTIONS

- In what areas of your life are you influenced by monism? You might think of the authority structures in your life, or your role as child, parent, student or teacher. What about the differences between sexes? (See Genesis 1:27; Romans 13:1–5; Ephesians 5:22–33; 6:1–4.)

- How can Christians balance their responsibilities to the democratic system with their commitment to Christian truth and morals? (See Romans 13:1–4; Acts 5:27–32.)

- How does Christian commitment apply to issues like school prayer and homosexual civil rights?

- What would happen to society if all these distinctions were eliminated? Would it be heaven on earth or a totalitarian nightmare?

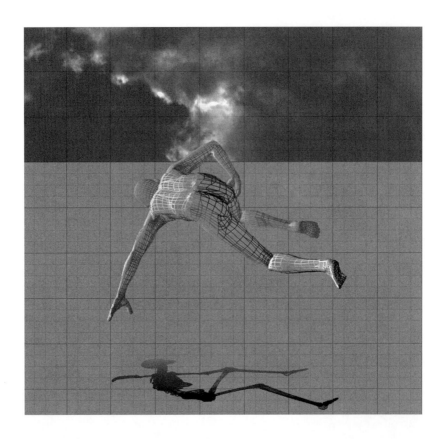

GOSPEL TRUTH 4

One problem: death through sin

Some time ago, an unusual event took place that caused the Japanese people to live in daily fear. A strange religious cult had left a few drops of the deadly gas, sarin, in the subway system, which threatened to kill thousands. Imagine if I offered you a glass of water and told you that there was only one drop of sarin in it; otherwise, the water was perfectly pure. Oh, sarin is not pleasant, but what could one drop do? Would you accept my logic? Yet we argue that a few drops of sin in our lives don't make us sinful. The Bible shows sin to be as deadly and toxic on a spiritual level as sarin is on a physical level. A few drops are enough to take down the whole race.

The monists call for us to wake up. So does the Bible. 'Wake up, O sleeper, rise from the dead' (Ephesians 5:14). The Bible wakes us not from ignorance but 'from the dead'. The day human beings rebelled against God's authority at the beginning of time, the poison of sin entered the fountain of life and turned its waters toxic. The natural state of man is not the circle of life but the circle of death. We are alienated from God, enemies—blind, foolish, and evil. The human heart is desperately wicked, full of corruption, and only evil continually (Genesis 6:5). This is not the picture of an innocent lion cub, like Simba, asleep to his real nature.

Our hearts need conversion, not awakening. If we stir the human heart to life without the transformation of God's Holy Spirit, it will only spew forth evil, hatred and deception. Even our best efforts at humanitarian good are about as attractive as dirty laundry (Isaiah 64:6)! No act of love is acceptable to God unless it is done by his power and for his glory.

Pagans believe that making distinctions is sin. The Bible teaches the very opposite. The original sin is the refusal of divine distinctions, in particular, the first distinction of all, the absolute distinction between the Creator and the creature. Here is how it goes. The clever serpent insinuates that the Creator's word is ambiguous ('Did God really say?') and therefore hardly dependable. Eve falls for the lie that in order to be free, she must make her own, independent choices, and create her own world. Eve chooses to believe the pagan/diabolical lie that if she relies on herself, if she goes within, she can be divine.

Only the Creator knows what the creation should look like. Only God knows what true purity is. He places all the distinctions in the creation he made in order to remind us of that first great distinction which should bring us humbly to our knees before him. All other sins are consequences of the refusal of that first distinction.

To destroy the distinction between sin and goodness allows us to ease our consciences. But somewhere underneath, we still recognize objective evil. We know that two eleven-year-olds dropping a five-year-old from a fourth floor apartment window is evil. We know that cruel dictators who gas their own citizens are evil. Even more important, we recognize as evil the rage and selfishness we see when we look honestly into our own hearts.

But how *do* we deal with this evil? Do we embrace it, accept it, come to love it? Or do we fall on our knees and recognize our need for God's grace, confessing with the church 'grace alone':

Sola Gratia

QUESTIONS

- How do you think you could convince your non-Christian friend that our problem is not that we are asleep? (See Ezekiel 37; Ephesians 2:1–2; 5:14.)

- What part does conscience play in the realization of sin? Is conscience infallible? (See Romans 1:18–20; 1 Corinthians 4:3–5; 1 John 1:8–10; 3:18–24.)

- Do you think conscience can be stamped out in a person's heart? (See Psalm 19:1–4; 1 Timothy 4:1–2.)

- List some historical examples of wilful evil. Think of examples in your own experience.

- What happens to a society when evil is considered as mere forgetfulness? (See Hosea 5:14–16.)

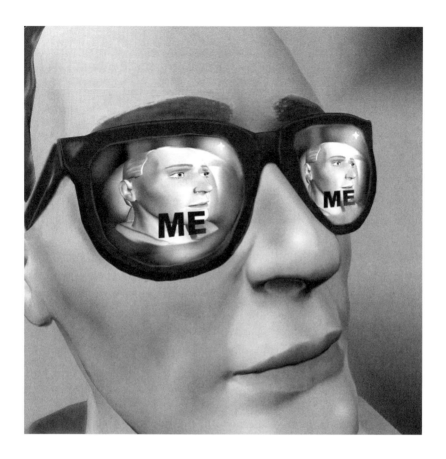

PAGAN LIE 5

One escape: look within

In *Lion King*, the young Simba, distressed by conflict and a lack of identity, lies in a field contemplating the stars. Thanks to the deep, mystical wisdom of Rafiki, the witch-doctor, Simba experiences a coming of age. He has a father/mother-earth revelation and identifies the stars, and later his own reflection in a pool, as his father.

Monists tell us to complete the circle by looking into ourselves. Your self sits at the centre. Spiritual understanding dawns when you eliminate distinctions and rational controls to take your place in the unity of all things.

Sixties rebels discovered themselves through drugs. Today, meditation has replaced dangerous drugs as the path to the discovery of self and God. Meditation allows you to detach from your body's limitations and discover a connection with the whole through a mystical experience of true knowledge (*gnosis*). As more individuals find their divine identity, the planet will, it is believed, shift into a unified, altered state of consciousness.

But there is more to a spiritual high than trancelike ecstasy. Going beyond the limitations of the mind also goes beyond rational definitions of right and wrong. Everything about you is OK. All your instincts are valid. As the sixties hippies said: 'If it feels good, do it.' Or, as C. G. Jung said, our instincts are spiritual *archetypes*, or powers, that we must accept in order to be fully integrated persons. When we go within, notions like right and wrong, guilt and bad conscience disappear. By embracing evil, pagan spirituality produces a temporary, counterfeit euphoria of *virtual redemption*.

I once developed a painful ear infection. The specialist took a tool called a strawberry, inserted it into my ear, and punctured an abscess. The pain went away, but so did some of my hearing—for ever! Conscience is as delicate as hearing. Those who mess with it have, in the words of Paul, a 'conscience seared as with a hot iron' (1 Timothy 4:2).

The powerful experience of embracing evil can sometimes appear more attractive than the mundane faithfulness of genuine Christian living in the real world of good and evil. Such liberation from self-doubt, we are told, holds the key to the planet's spiritual future. People are discovering their divine, guilt-free identity. In a Los Angeles public school, a teacher told her children: 'Imagine that you are doing something perfect ... Imagine you are full of light. Now feel peace because you are perfect, intelligent, magnificent—because all the wisdom of the universe is within you.'

Subjective mystical experience has become the ideal for spirituality. Even Christians feel dissatisfied or guilty because their daily obedience doesn't seem spiritual enough. They hanker for a deep, mystical knowledge that takes them to a higher level. They look to their own experience as a proof of their salvation or spiritual growth.

If you identify certain emotional or physical experiences as signs of your salvation, instead of trusting in Christ's death and resurrection, beware of slipping into Simba's trance. Your longing for perfect communion with God is good. The longing itself is created by God's Spirit, and if you have placed your faith in Christ, you know the taste of faith, of love, of hope and of peace produced by communion with God. The Spirit will give you the faith to persevere in obedience, and to wait patiently for the day we no longer see God 'through a glass darkly' (1 Corinthians 13:12). One day we will see him face to face and be utterly fulfilled.

While my new grandson was in his mother's womb, he could sense her presence. She carried him, cared for him, loved him. But he could not look into her face until he had gone through the dark tunnel of the birth canal and burst into the light of day. Only then could he stare into her eyes and know her. One day we will pass through the dark waters of death and come out in the light of heaven. Only then will we look right into Christ's eyes, finally free from our bondage to sin, finally able to know full intimacy with our dear Lord. Until then, we must not be tricked by false promises of intimacy with God which may only take us deeper into our own sin. As in childbirth, there's no way out but through!

QUESTIONS

- Does the Bible ever recommend that believers seek altered states of consciousness as a means of spiritual contact with God? (See Romans 12:1–2; 1 Corinthians 2:10–16; 2 Corinthians 10:3–5.)

- Does the Bible ever support the use of drugs for the same purpose? (See Galatians 5:20; Revelation 9:21; 18:23; 21:8; 22:15. Note that the Greek term, *pharmakia*, which occurs in these verses, is translated as 'sorcery,' 'witchcraft,' or 'magic potion'.)

- Does the Bible ever suggest that we bypass the mind in order to experience deep contact with God? (See 1 John 4:1–3 as well as the references in the first question.)

- Is it significant that, in the Bible, God is never presented as a goddess?

- How crucial is the period of the sixties for this radical change in spiritual thinking?

GOSPEL TRUTH 5

One escape: look to Him

When my eldest daughter was three, she had stitches removed from her chin. As she sat, petrified, on the edge of the doctor's table, I watched her look into my wife's face. The absolute trust, love, and dependence that showed in her deep blue eyes remains engraved in my memory. It is that look of confidence and love that we owe to God. That intent gaze will save us as we look to our God to take out the stitches of sin. Jesus said that to enter the kingdom of God we must become like little children, looking by faith into the face of Christ.

But pagans scorn the need to turn to the God of the Bible. According to Christianity, such dependence on God is the only possible solution. Pagans turn within, which the Bible declares to be the essence of sin and the height of folly. These two solutions can hardly be more contradictory. Christians turn to Christ, the almighty Creator and Redeemer (Colossians 1:15–20), because turning to him who made the heavens and the earth and who has the power to redeem them, is both right and wise.

When I was a young man of twenty-nine, I was tormented by a deep sense of unworthiness. Though I had grown up in a Christian home, and was in the middle of a Ph.D. in theology, I would wake each morning with a sick feeling in the pit of my stomach, caused by the horror of my insecurity.

One day was different. Unable to function, I realized that I was at the end of my resources. My attempts to resolve my sinful, fearful past had all failed. In a situation of utter desperation, I reached out to Christ. I fixed my mind's eye on the Son of God, and saw him as he hung dying on the cross because of my sin. With an overwhelming sense that this act was for me, no strings attached, I fell off to sleep.

The next morning was the first day of the rest of my life, and it was different, because I leaped out of bed with the verse of a hymn on my lips:

Nothing in my hand I bring, Simply to thy cross I cling.
Naked come to thee for dress, Helpless look to thee for grace.
Foul, I to the fountain fly. Wash me, Saviour, or I die.

By the powerful work of God's life-giving Spirit, I was alive, and every morning since then has been the same—so gloriously different.
Christians turn to Christ for the only satisfactory solution to personal sin and guilt. Because it is God's solution, there is real deliverance from the torment of a bad conscience. This is the incredibly *good news* of the Gospel. Deliverance comes not from embracing one's evil as good. It comes from falling down before Christ's cross,

for here true and unique satisfaction is made for sin. Christ the sinless one bears our sins by dying for us at a particular time and in a particular place in human history. At that moment, the price of our sin is paid. Our account before God is wiped clean as we confess, not embrace, our sins, and as we put on the robe of Christ's righteousness. In the whole of human history this is the only transaction that satisfies God's—and even our—standard of justice.

Everyone believes in redemption, but views of redemption differ dramatically. The pagans believe that redemption is *liberation from* the Creator. Christians believe redemption is *reconciliation with* the Creator, through his saving acts. According to Gospel truth, you can do nothing—except hold out your hand. God does everything. The Father, in love, conceives of redemption; the Son, in submission, accomplishes it; and the Holy Spirit, in power, applies it to unworthy human hearts—by raising the dead body of Jesus from the grave, and by giving to believers the first instalment of their future resurrection life. Can you create a fabulously complex physical universe like the one in which we live? Can you raise a dead body to life, or deal with your own sin? If you're honest, you know the answer is 'No!' You need the God of the gospel. The two events of creation and resurrection define our past, our present and our future. Pagan lies can never duplicate them.

By knowing the almighty God of the Bible and his loving acts for us, we discover who we really are—redeemed creatures entirely dependent on the Creator's love. The first great truth we learn about ourselves is the distinction between the Creator and the creature. This is what I call two-ism. Existence is made up of two kinds of beings: God, the personal triune Creator,and everything else, which is creation. This is the essential distinction which is reflected in the way God makes the world. This first distinction is thus both true and life-giving. All the other God-created distinctions (some of which you will discover on the following pages) are also true and life-giving because that is the way God made the world. Accepting our place within them, we give glory to God, Creator and Redeemer. The treasure of the gospel is expressed in earthen, created vessels (2 Corinthians 4:7). Reconciled with the Creator, who is distinct from us but intimately related to us by his grace, we receive his distinctions and live them with joyful thanksgiving as we await the new heaven and earth.

CREATOR/CREATURE

For the health of the planet and the good of mankind, God must rule over his creation, and creatures must submit to his design. When God is eliminated, as in today's pagan view of ecology, things go haywire. As a leading earth-worshipping feminist says, 'Nature would be much better off without us.' How different from the Bible, which gives mankind lordship and stewardship over the earth. In the world God created, he places structures that remind us that he cannot be confused with the things he made.

GOD/MAN

'The fear of the Lord is the beginning of wisdom' (Proverbs 9:10) illustrates the theistic character of the Bible. If existence is two, we need God's revelation of himself. Our search for wisdom discovers a God outside creation, the uncreated one, who reveals himself through his Word. One of the church's great confessions asks: 'What is man's chief end?' and answers: 'to glorify God and to enjoy him for ever.' Understanding the correct relationship between man and God is essential for human enjoyment. If the creation was made to bring glory to God, man will not find satisfaction in worshipping it. Only the 'fear of the Lord' gives creation deep significance and provokes in human beings the deep desire to love and care for what God made 'good'.

ANIMAL/HUMAN

A leading teacher of ethics at Princeton University, author of many books on animal rights, argues that a one month old baby is no more valuable than a snail! If there are no distinctions, human beings will be treated like animals, and animals like humans. The God of the Bible has lovingly ordered the world: animals serve humanity, which symbolizes the way human beings should serve God. Animals witness to God's creative power. Humans respond with wise stewardship of everything God has made for their good.

RIGHT/WRONG

When right and wrong are present, as in the biblical worldview of two-ism, moral life is possible, human existence is meaningful and society is preserved. Without this distinction, society disintegrates. True spiritual experience is based on righteousness, not on sin.

LIFE/DEATH

Scripture denounces death as a horrible blight on the creation. It is 'the last enemy', a real expression of evil that has been vanquished by Christ's resurrection. Ignorance of this fact produces woeful delusion.

CHRIST/SATAN

Knowing Christ gives hope of eternal life: Satan is the deceiver, masquerading as an 'angel of light', but really a devouring lion.

Making this distinction is crucial for spiritual survival. We do not welcome Antichrist, but resist him, standing firm in the faith. Jesus himself shows us how to defend against Satan's wiles, and that is by living from every word that comes from the mouth of God. The Christian's best defence against counterfeit christs is to know the Christ of the Scriptures.

HEAVEN/HELL

If you were in a small boat, unaware of deadly rapids a mile downstream, and a local on the bank failed to tell you, his would be a scandalous silence. Some countries would consider that silence a crime—'non-assistance to persons in danger'. Knowing about heaven and hell and their eternal consequences is essential if mankind is to find an escape from spiritual danger. Christians who warn their friends about the existence of hell are not proud or self-righteous. They are throwing a line to those sailing headlong towards the rapids.

SIN/HOLINESS

To solve our problem, we need to know the truth about sin. 'The wages of sin is death' (Romans 6:23). It is also true that without holiness no one will see God. These are crucial notions. Because we are sinners, only Christ's holiness, which covers us when we trust in his sacrifice for us, will allow us to 'see God'. Our sin will only lead to social and eternal disaster.

ORTHODOXY/HERESY

There is a right belief and a wrong belief, even if the wrong belief pretends to be Christian. As the Apostle Paul says, with great emphasis, 'If anybody preaches to you a gospel other than what you accepted, let him be eternally condemned' (Galatians 1:9).

THE BIBLE/OTHER SCRIPTURES

However much worldly wisdom might be contained in the various religious traditions, the Bible is the only written text that is 'God-breathed', from the God who is outside the creation, and thus is the only scripture able to 'make wise unto salvation' (2 Timothy 3:15).

CHRISTIANITY/PAGANISM

The Bible condemns false forms of the Christian faith, but opposes even more vigorously non-Christian religions, both in the Old and New Testaments. In the Old we read: 'The Israelites did evil in the eyes of the LORD; they forgot the LORD their God and served the Baals and the Asherahs' (Judges 3:7). Paul has equally stern words for Christians tempted to participate in pagan ceremonies: 'The sacrifices of pagans [their religious devotions] are offered to demons, not to God' (1 Corinthians 10:20). There is no common ground, in spite of the call from radical 'Christian' theologians to 'pass over' into the spirituality of non-Christian religions in order to experience 'true' spirituality and tolerance. The Bible is unambiguous: 'You cannot drink the cup of the Lord and the cup of demons' (1 Corinthians 10:21).

MALE/FEMALE

Just after its account of the creation of man, the Bible makes the first great distinction: the difference between male and female: 'So God created man in his own image; in the image of God he created him; male and female he created them' (Genesis 1:27). As the French say: 'Vive la différence!' Male-and-female perpetuates the human race and expresses both difference and communion. Heterosexuality is a forceful reminder of the theistic character of creation. The Bible has no place for alternate genders. Heterosexuality is a reflection of theism, just as homosexuality and bisexuality are expressions of pagan monism (Romans 1:24-25).

TRADITIONAL FAMILY/ALTERNATE FAMILY

Maintaining the Bible's patriarchal, heterosexual family model honours God, the great Patriarch, and preserves society. This family is the essential building block of a mature civilization. Whenever it is abandoned, social collapse quickly follows. The love of a father who protects his wife and children, reflects God's love for his children. The love of a man for his wife reflects the love of Christ for his church. It is not because sinners abuse the structure that it ceases to show us a glimpse of God's future heavenly family.

CHILD/PARENT

The Bible presents a beautiful picture of the obedient, happy child, and of the loving, responsible parent, in which the roles are not confused and the expectations are clear. Such an order is not only fundamental to the mental and spiritual health of the family as God created it, but also expresses something profound about the person of the triune God, who reveals himself specifically as wise Father, loving Son, and powerful Spirit (Ephesians 6:1–4).

AUTHORITY/SUBMISSION

People often hate authority, yet it is essential to the way God made us, and to the way in which he put together all these enriching distinctions. Authority structures are a part of the variety of creation, of God's rich palette of colours. There is nothing degrading about submission. Just as the Son submitted himself to the loving Father to gain for us salvation and one day will make himself subject to God the Father (1 Corinthians 15:24–28), so we submit to one another—citizens to rulers (Romans 13:1–15), wives to husbands (Ephesians 5:22ff), children to parents (Ephesians 6:1–4), employees to employers (Ephesians 6:5-9) and the Church to Christ (Ephesians 5:24).

The final solution is not the destruction of these created distinctions but their resurrection/transformation in God's new heaven and earth. As we await the final, transforming miracle of the resurrection, we should know that the Christian life is not always outwardly spectacular. The Bible is down-to-earth and disarmingly honest. Paul describes the Christian stance in the world this way: 'I consider that our present sufferings are not to be compared with the glory that will be revealed in us' (Romans 8:18). Jesus promises that Christians will be hated and persecuted, as he was. Though we all long for a full spirituality that satisfies us completely, we will not experience perfect peace and joy until the last battle with the great liar and deceiver is over and Christ returns to welcome us into the home he has prepared for us. In the meantime, we are called to faithful obedience in the concrete, everyday struggles of life, being faithful to God, our Creator and Redeemer, in the distinctions he has made. Knowing and loving God is the pearl of greatest price, the treasure we now have in earthen vessels, without which life would be meaningless.

With that treasure in our hand, we live by faith in what God has already done when he raised Jesus from the dead, and in what he will do when we and all creation will be transformed (Romans 8:22–25). As the Bible says, in this life 'we walk by faith …' (2 Corinthians 5:7):

Sola Fide

QUESTIONS

- Is the maintaining of distinctions peripheral or essential to the Christian witness to Gospel truth in this most confusing of times? (See Genesis 1:6–7, 14, 17,18, 27; Matthew 19:4; 2 Corinthians 6:14–17; Ephesians 5:22–6:4, 12.)
- Will there be distinctions in heaven? (See Matthew 22:30; 1 Corinthians 2:9, 15:28; Rev. 21:1; 22:5.)
- Why do you think the Bible describes heaven as a marriage feast (Revelation 21:2-3)? (See Matthew 5:8; 1 Corinthians 13:12; 1 John 3:2–3.)

Gospel truth, pagan lies and you

In the spiritual domain, these two options are the only ones available. Neutrality is impossible, so decision time is upon you. The only real question you ever have to ask yourself is: who am I? You will have one of three answers: 1. You will put your head into the sand and deny the spiritual challenge. 2. You will look to the god within you and try to convince yourself that you are god. 3. You will look outside yourself to the God who made you and everything around you, whom you can never be, but whom you can know through Jesus. That answer will be: I am a sinful creature but redeemed by my loving Creator

Hopefully, you can now recognize the difference between Gospel truth and pagan lies, truth and falsehood. But you need to answer one more question and it's a question you can't answer with a superficial sentence or two in a group discussion. That question is, 'Where do *you* stand?'

In the quiet moments of your heart, do you seek communion with your higher, divine self, and try to convince yourself that the evil in your own heart is really good? Or do you detest your own sin and look into the disfigured but beautiful face of Jesus as your only hope of true justice, real forgiveness and perfect love?

One day, you will stand before God, your Judge. If you are still looking within, you will be covered with shame, and you will no longer be able to avoid the burning gaze of a holy God. However, if you humbly look to Christ for mercy now, and receive the gift he offers you of full and free salvation, you will be able to stand before God's throne and look your Creator and Judge in the eye, for that eye will see in you the beauty of Jesus' perfection and will not turn away from you. You will hear a word of total acceptance: 'Well done, good, faithful servant. Enter into my rest' (Matthew 25:21).

If you are already a Christian, I hope this booklet will clarify the battle lines for you. And if, by reading it, by taking a look at ground zero theology, you have discovered to your surprise that you would have to consider yourself a pagan, then I pray that you will open your heart to the personal God who reaches out in love to you through his Son Jesus. He made you and the earth on which you live. He placed you where you are right now, and even caused you to be reading these lines.

He is a true Father, tender, strong, and full of love. He has promised that if you seek him you will find him. He offers you his true love. Look to his Word to discover who he is and turn away from the deception of your own heart, from the pagan lies you have believed. You will find a pure and holy Saviour to wash you clean and dress you in new clothes, for Jesus says: 'Come to me, and I will give you rest' (Matthew 11:28).

SUMMARY: PAGAN LIES

1. ALL IS ONE AND ONE IS ALL

God is the Spirit of everything. Man, animals, rocks and trees are all god. There is no major distinction between God and Man.

2. HUMANITY IS ONE

If all people are equal, no group has unique access to the truth. All humans are divine and must live together, accepting a common standard of morality and trying to become as much like one another as possible, rather than emphasizing distinctions that can cause friction.

3. ALL RELIGIONS ARE ONE

No religion knows the only path to God. All roads lead to the top of the mountain, from which we see the same moon. Religions should emphasize their similarities, not their differences, since they share the same mystical experience.

4. ONE PROBLEM: AMNESIA

Since God is in all of us, is all of us, we should not worry about sin and guilt. If we wake up to the wonderful reality that we are God, we will eliminate the distinctions of sex, role and doctrine that divide us.

5. ONE ESCAPE: LOOK WITHIN

If you want to be happy, you need to love yourself, and stop feeling guilty. The more you believe in yourself and your own power—the more you assert that power for your own happiness, the sooner you will have a sense of freedom from constraint. You will enjoy a truly peaceful and fulfilled experience of God.

SUMMARY: GOSPEL TRUTH

1. ONE GOD, THE CREATOR

Everything that is not God was created by him: the earth, animals and man, who alone is in his image. God is distinct from his creation.

2. ONE IN CHRIST ALONE

The only true unity is created by common faith in Jesus Christ. God defines two categories of people: his children and those who are in rebellion against him. True Christian love knows no racial or economic barriers.

3. ONE TRUTH

Jesus says we can only approach the Father through him. Christians do not revere Christ as one great prophet among others. He is God in human form, come to rescue us from our sin. To spiritualize him as a christ, present in a variety of religions, is to refuse him.

4. ONE PROBLEM: DEATH THROUGH SIN

Sin has ruined our peace with God. We dare not approach him because he is so pure that we would be destroyed. Yet sin also destroys us. Without God's solution, the problem of sin is insurmountable.

5. ONE ESCAPE: LOOK TO HIM

God comes to save us. We do not have to find salvation in the dark recesses of our hearts. We can admit the reality of our sin, repent, and receive God's just forgiveness. Jesus became sin for us and took its guilt and punishment. He then proved his power over sin in his resurrection. He will transform us and receive us as his children to live with him for ever.

No one can serve two lords; either he will hate the one and love the other, or he will be loyal to the one and despise the other. You cannot serve God and earthly things.
**The words of Jesus,
Matthew 6:24**

BY THE SAME AUTHOR:

The Gnostic Empire Strikes Back: AN OLD HERESY FOR A NEW AGE

Spirit Wars: PAGAN REVIVAL IN CHRISTIAN AMERICA

Capturing the Pagan Mind: PAUL'S BLUEPRINT FOR THINKING AND LIVING IN THE NEW GLOBAL CULTURE

Cracking the Da Vinci Code: SEPARATING FACT FROM FICTION
CO-AUTHOR, JAMES GARLOW

The God of sex: HOW SPIRITUALITY DETERMINES YOUR SEXUALITY

Stolen Identity: CONSPIRACY TO REINVENT JESUS

Order at your local bookstore, or on-line at: www.cwipp.org

ALSO IN THIS SERIES

WHAT THE BIBLE SAYS ABOUT GOING OUT, MARRIAGE AND SEX

CHRIS RICHARDS AND LIZ JONES

God calls us to follow him in every area of our lives, including our sexuality. We were beautifully, delicately, intricately created as sexual beings, but we are so quickly marred when we disregard God's instructions. In a clear biblical and medical framework, two medical doctors sensitively address the matter of relationships.

'Dr Chris Richards and Dr Liz Jones have dared to tell it is as it is, by honestly and frankly explaining what the Bible teaches on sex and relationships.'
ROGER CARSWELL

64PP, BOOKLET, ILLUSTRATED, £3,   ISBN 978 1 903087 87 9

UNIVERSITY—THE REAL CHALLENGE

ANDREW KING

Is university a good thing for young Christians? Is it a great maturing process, a time of spiritual growth and evangelism? Or is it a time of overwhelming worldly influence, compromise and drifting away from God? Practical pointers to students, parents and churches.

64PP, BOOKLET, ILLUSTRATED, £3,   ISBN 978 1 903087 82 4

A CUP OF COLD WATER

JULIA JONES

As Julia Jones looks thoughtfully at this subject, you will see that food plays only a small part and that hospitality can be as simple as tea and biscuits, or a cold drink on a hot day. Through true hospitality, relationships between Christians can be wonderfully deepened. Careful consideration is given to such matters as the biblical basis for giving hospitality, why some people find it hard to show hospitality, what hospitality 'looks like', how to get ready for it, and how to exercise hospitality with sensitivity.

64PP, BOOKLET, ILLUSTRATED, £3,   978 1 84625 020 0